Learning to Read
is Child's Play
for Parents

Published by
Crossbridge Books, Worcester
www.crossbridgeeducational.com
Copyright © Crossbridge Books 2020

All rights reserved
No part of this publication may be reproduced,
stored in a retrieval system or transmitted in
any form or by any means— electronic, mechanical,
photocopying, recording or otherwise—without
prior permission of the copyright owner.

ISBN 978-1-8380028-7-9

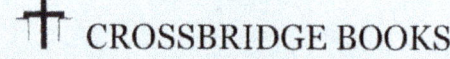 CROSSBRIDGE BOOKS

Learning to Read is Child's Play

for Parents

by

Dr Ruth Price-Mohr

CONTENTS		Page
Introduction		1
Chapter 1	In the beginning	2
Chapter 2	Getting started	7
Chapter 3	Taking the next step	15
Chapter 4	Games and activities	23
Chapter 5	Using books	27
Chapter 6	Next steps	31

Introduction

This is a book that I have long wanted to write. It is intended for parents from all communities and languages. There will be a companion book for teachers, and those with responsibility for the care and development of children, that will include all the relevant academic references, but I have kept this book free from such distractions. What I share here is based on decades of experience and research, both my own and that of others recognised and respected internationally.

There was a time when only the privileged had the opportunity to learn to read, but in today's world the ability to read has become a necessity. As society has changed and the purpose for reading has changed, so has the way it has been taught, and in the process many myths have emerged, often promoted by political or economic interests. I have no wish to discuss the history of teaching reading in this book – that is for another volume. The approach shared here is based on the simple fact that learning to read is child's play; it is not rocket science and everyone can do it.

Chapter 1 – In the beginning

On the day your child was born, he or she had already learned to recognise your voice and probably the voices of others living in the same household. During the first few weeks after birth, your baby learnt to recognise your face, and we know that by three months of age, babies can recognise the difference between faces. Think about how much information your baby must be taking in to recognise faces; how much information do they use to recognise the difference between their cuddly toys? What about cars, pets, animals, dinosaurs, furniture, food and so on? Your child learns to recognise all these everyday things just from having them named, and written-words (on card) can be learned the same way.

So you could begin naming word-cards at the same time that you start to name other things in your baby's world. While your child is still learning to speak, they learn to understand much more of your language than you might realise, and by you naming the objects for them, eventually they will be able to copy you and begin naming things themselves; printed words (word-cards) are just other objects to young children that can be named.

I am not suggesting that you try to teach your tiny baby to read, but you can begin when your child begins to speak words aloud, although I have found that children of about eighteen months seem to enjoy it most. Yes, I did say enjoy – when words are shown to children and named as part of games, they naturally enjoy playing the games with you and pick up the names of the words incidentally without even being aware of it. The more fun the game, and the more attention they have from you, the easier they learn the names of the words.

You might ask me why I call it 'naming' the words rather than reading. The first step to understanding written script is that it is made up of individual words just like speech; at this stage these words are images that they see, just like images of your face or a toy. If you think of your role as 'naming' the words like objects, you will be less tempted to try to 'teach' your child to read. The first thing for your child to learn is that this thing is a word-card named, for example, 'mummy' and it is not a cuddly toy. The next thing for your child to learn is that there can be more than one type of word-card and that they are different, for example 'this one is mummy' and 'this one is daddy'. Then you can gradually name new word-cards, using words that matter - that are important - to your child.

You might also ask why you should start so early; why not wait till your child starts school and leave it to the professionals? There's no reason why you should or should not. But there are enormous benefits if you do. Firstly, it gives you another activity to do with your child, and in my experience the children really enjoy the activities, especially when they have your undivided attention. Secondly, it supports their developing speech, helping them to hear the whole word and to recognise more easily where words in speech begin and end. Thirdly, it makes learning to read so much easier; your child won't even remember when or how they learned to read, and will be well ahead of their peers when they start school, making it easier for them to give more attention to getting to know their new friends.

Below is some feedback from two parents who participated in the original Child's Play Project during which this approach was successfully used:

"Thanks to Ruth's help, both our children are reading far beyond their expected age range. This skill was taught prior to primary school in a very relaxed and fun way allowing the children to have a wonderful head start to their school life. Reading a book is a joy for the children, not a struggle, and this in turn helps with learning and understanding new skills both at home and at school. My husband and I, but ultimately the children (even though they don't know it), are extremely grateful for all that Ruth has done for them."

"My daughter has been doing the child's Play project for three and a half years. It was a great way to introduce her to reading and learning words before she started school and a great tool to use alongside the reading she did at school. She has just finished year 1 and is doing brilliantly. Ruth made the word games really interesting for little ones, it was a fun way to learn new words and worked in line with the Weebee reading series. The Weebee reading books were lovely and the Weebee characters were great. My daughter grew quite an attachment to them (as did I!) and we are sad to say goodbye to them."

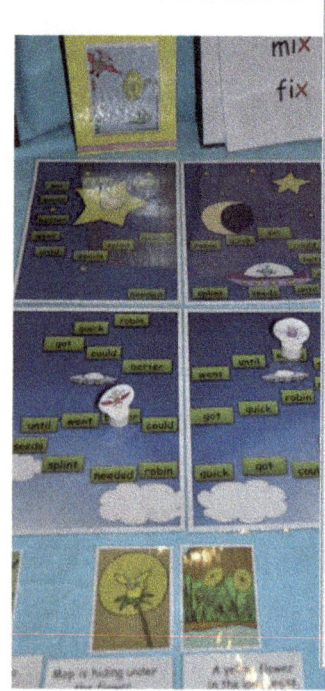
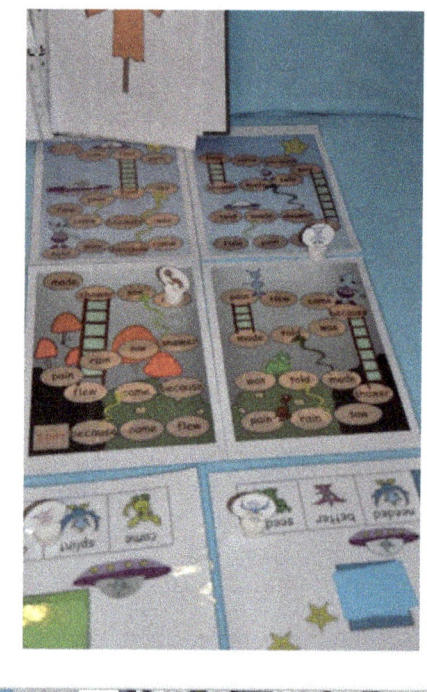

Chapter 2 – Getting started

The first step

- Choosing the first word
- Choosing the first six words
- Choosing subsequent sets of six words

Choosing the first word

The first word needs to be the most important person or object in your child's life. This is most likely to be your child's own name, but could be the name of the main care-giver or the name of a favourite toy.

- Present the word on a plain piece of card (you can use the inside of a cereal box).
- Write the word in lower case letters (not capitals).
- Each letter should be approximately 8cm high.
- Write the words in red with thick lines as shown below.

mummy

Notebook

Keep a record of your child's first six words here.

'Naming' the first word

To 'name' the word, wait for a moment when your child is happy and busy. Then show the word-card and speak it clearly and with great enthusiasm (think of an advertising slogan). Hold it up for about 10 seconds and then put it down until the following day. Repeat this for about a week. You can leave the word-card somewhere near the toy box; you want your child to think of the word as just another object to play with and name.

Choosing the first six words

You now need to choose another five words. These need to be important to your child, for example members of the family, pet names or favourite toys. During the second week, add one new word and during the next weeks add one word per week. Remember to show each word with great enthusiasm and speak it in a clear voice as if you were selling something. Show each word for no more than 10 seconds each. Don't try to get your child to copy you, when he or she is ready to, they will. Resist the temptation to test your child - recognising and naming an object can be done in your head - it is not the same thing as speaking it aloud.

Questions and answers:

- **Q**: Does the order matter?
- **A**: No, if your child prefers an order let them have it.

- **Q**: Can they play with the words?
- **A**: Yes, if you have laminated the words or they are on very strong card, if not you need to beware of them chewing bits off and accidently swallowing – it could cause choking.

- **Q**: Can I make words in a second language?
- **A**: Yes, if your child is learning to speak in more than one language.

- **Q**: Can we use emotions like the word happy?
- **A**: Yes, if the words are important to your child.

Choosing the next words

You will need to choose another six words; remember that these words need to have meaning for your child. If they can be names of familiar objects (for example cat or dog or a favourite toy) this will make the games easier in the future.

Naming the next six words

Over the next six weeks, just continue to add one new word per week. Keep to words that have meaning for your child. Each new word needs to be the same colour and font size. If you are printing from a word document use 200 point size, alternatively you could use a wide-tipped felt pen, crayons, or even a paint brush. Always show the words with great enthusiasm and for no more than 10 seconds. They can be spread out over the day, just two or three at a time or all at once depending on how your child responds.

There should now be twelve word-cards in your child's collection. If you feel your child wants to move at a faster pace, let them.

Notebook

Keep a record of your child's next six words here.

Questions and answers:

- **Q**: Can we use names?
- **A**: Yes, names are good words to use.

- **Q**: Should we continue with all the words on a daily basis?
- **A**: You don't need to do all the words every day. The early words are best looked at every now and again so that they are not forgotten.

- **Q:** If my child asks me about a letter (maybe picked up from preschool or nursery) do I say the name of the letter or the sound?
- **A:** Both. For example: "Yes, it's the letter M (em) and it makes the sound 'mmm'".

Chapter 3 – Taking the next step

The next steps

- Moving to black and white
- Changing font size

Moving to black and white

Starting with the first word-card, make a copy in black lettering. This needs to look the same as the original but in black as shown below.

mummy

Copy one word per day into black in the same order that they were first used. This step is important as most books print words in black and they need to learn that colour is not relevant to the name of a word-card.

TIP: When your child finds the word-card you have asked for cheer and applause – do this as often as you can, they love it!

Notebook

Keep a record of the words as you change them to black.

Naming the first six words in black

To begin with, just randomly mix and match the words as you show them. After a few days, you can try a little matching game. Lay the black words out on the floor, hold up one of the original red words and ask your child to show you the word on the floor. If your child shows no interest in this just continue holding up the words as before.

If your child enjoys this game, you can extend it by hiding the black words around the room and playing 'hunt the matching word'. When you feel your child is happy with just recognising the black words, put the red words away and just keep the black words out. You can then convert your second set of word-cards into black.

Remember: never test your child and never let your child get bored or disinterested – stop before that happens!

Once your first set of twelve words has been converted into black lettering you can begin with some new words. Introduce another six words, one per day. This time use a different colour for each word. During the following weeks convert these to black lettering, no more than one per day.

Photo album

Post your own photos here

Changing font size

Without introducing any new words, begin to reduce the font size. Start with the oldest words first. Make a set of cards for the first six words, approximately 5cm high and each in a different colour. Make a matching set in black as shown below.

| mummy |

| mummy |

The following week do the same for your second set of six words, and the next week for your third set of six words. You should now have two sets of the eighteen word-cards in your child's collection in a smaller size; one set in different colours and one set in black.

TIP: Remember to cheer and applause.

Notebook

Keep a record as you change to different colours.

Photo album

Post your own photos here

Chapter 4 – Games and activities

Games to play with the eighteen word-cards
- Word matching
- Hunt the word
- Hunt the object

Word matching

Lay out all the words from both sets of the smaller font. Put the coloured words neatly in rows of six with spaces underneath. Ask your child to find the matching black words and put them underneath the coloured words. Start with your first six words and gradually increase until your child can find all eighteen easily and quickly.

Hunt the word

Place the black words around the room. Give your child the coloured words one at a time and ask them to find the matching words. Start with the first six and gradually increase until you are using all eighteen.

Hunt the object

If any of the words in your child's collection represents an object, for example a teddy, give your child the word and ask them to find what it says (*not tell you what it says*).

Notebook

Make a note of all your ideas for games here.

More ideas

Put the words into a story. As you tell the story, hold up a word that will fit in and ask your child to say the word as part of telling the story. For example "One day (mummy) went to the (shop) to buy just one (banana) for her little monster…."

Choose another set of six words and this time deliberately choose words for the hunt-the-object game, for example book, box, button, bear, ball, bat. Try to find a set of words that all start with the same letter. There should now be twenty four words in your child's collection.

Remember to start with red lettering 10cm high for new words and replace with black lettering after a week or so and then reduce the size.

Some more ideas:

- Hunt the words that begin with…
- Find all the names
- Find all the toys

TIP: Remember to cheer and applause.

Chapter 5 – Using books

Using books

- Importance of direction and tracking
- Orientation
- Familiar phrases

Direction and tracking

Books written in English follow the convention of words flowing in a left to right direction. In Arabic and Hebrew, writing goes from right to left; in ancient Chinese the script went from top to bottom; in ancient Greece they wrote left to right and then on the next line right to left. Why am I telling you this? So that you can see that babies are born with the capacity to read in any direction, but need to learn which direction is needed for their own particular language.

So when your child is sitting on your lap and you are reading their favourite stories, point to individual words while you read so they can follow the movement of your finger. You may not think that they notice, but they will follow the direction of your gaze and the direction of your finger without even being aware of it themselves. You don't need to say 'follow my finger' they will just do it.

Orientation

Another important element that your child will pick up from you when you read to them is orientation – which way up the book goes and of course which way up the words should be, and which way to turn the pages. These things might seem obvious to you but they are fundamental ground rules your child needs to learn and it won't take them long to pick it up so long as you show them.

Familiar phrases

Most of what happens in our day-to-day lives is predictable. Our speech is predictable and full of familiar predictable phrases. In the same way that a child can easily copy repeated familiar spoken phrases, such as 'bye bye' or 'night night', they can learn repeated familiar phrases from books such as 'once upon a time' or 'they lived happily ever after'. This ability to predict is essential for skilful reading later when children begin to go from recognising single words to reading sentences. Encourage your child to join in with you so that you read books together. When a book is familiar, wait for your child to fill in the gaps, or say the last word of a phrase, to encourage prediction.

Photo album

Post your own photos here

Chapter 6 – Next steps

Next steps

- Putting words together
- Preparing to read the first books
- Reading the first books

Putting words together

Your child will already understand about joining words together to make sentences in speech. They don't need any explanation but they will need to recognise those little words that we use for joining words to make sentences. In the same way you made all your first word-cards, make some that you can use to make sentences, for example:

- the
- and
- then
- this
- is

If you make several of each you will find it easier to make some simple sentences. You could use photos for ideas to go with the sentences, for example 'this is mummy and daddy' or 'this is the dinosaur'.

Notebook

Make a note of all the joining words you use.

Preparing to read the first books

The first books you use for your child to read themselves should ideally have just a few words on each page, and of course illustrations that clearly relate to the words. Make individual word-cards of all the words in the book; you may already have some of them in your collection. You need not worry if some of them seem long or complicated; children find it easier to recognise 'brontosaurus' than 'but'. Play all the usual games with the words to give your child a chance to 'name' them in the usual way.

Reading the first books

Now you can read the book together, giving your child the opportunity to point out words they recognise, fill in the gaps, or even tell you what it says themselves. You might be thinking 'this isn't reading, they are just remembering the words'; true, but this is how reading starts and the amazing thing about humans is that they can figure things out for themselves. If they don't know a word, name it for them, they will start to see patterns themselves. No explanations are needed – you can leave that bit to the teachers when they start school.

Photo album

Post your own photos here

The weebee books, and other reading books, used by families in the original Child's Play Project will be published by Crossbridge Books.

www.ingramcontent.com/pod-product-compliance
Lightning Source LLC
Chambersburg PA
CBHW071412160426
42813CB00085B/1079